A PRESERVATION GUIDE

Saving the Past and the Present for the Future

Barbara Sagraves

Ancestry

Sagraves, Barbara.

A preservation guide: saving the past and the present for the future / Barbara Sagraves

  p. cm.
Includes bibliographical references.
ISBN 0-916489-59-0 (pbk.)
1. Books—Conservation and restoration. 2. Paper—Preservation. 3. Photographs—Conservation and restoration. 4. Motion pictures—Conservation and restoration. 5. Sound recordings—Conservation and restoration. 6. Textile fabrics—Conservation and restoration. 7. Magnetic disks—Conservation and restoration. 8. Genealogy-Methodology. I. Title.
Z701.S24   1995
025.8'4-dc20   95-38059
                        CIP

First printing 1995
10 9 8 7 6 5 4 3 2 1

For other fine products from Ancestry, call or write:
ANCESTRY®
P.O. Box 476
Salt Lake City, UT 84110-0476
1-800 ANCESTRY
(1-800-262-3787)

◆ ◆ ◆

Contents

Foreword

The purpose of this guide is to provide guidelines for preserving books, manuscripts, photographs, audio- and videotapes, and other records collected or created during the course of genealogical research. The preservation treatments described are limited to those that can easily be performed by someone with no background or skill in conservation techniques. Special or more complex treatments should be carried out by trained and qualified conservators. (This guide includes guidelines for choosing such an individual.)

I would like to thank the staff of Northwestern University Library's Preservation Department, especially Deborah Howe, Giselle Simón, and Jane Welsh, for their advice and assistance. Any errors, either factual or by omission, are solely my responsibility.

Barbara Sagraves

(Photographs are courtesy of the author.)

General Guidelines for Storing Materials

What kinds of records might a researcher collect? They are many and varied:

- Paper: letters, newspaper clippings, legal documents, photocopies, computer printouts.
- Books: printed and manuscript.
- Photographs: color, black and white, negatives, slides, instant prints.
- Films: Super 8, 16mm, videotapes (both commercial and amateur).
- Sound recordings: phonograph records, audiotapes (cassettes, amateur recordings).
- Computer disks: commercial software, personal files.
- Textiles.

All of these items are subject to deterioration, which may occur chemically and/or physically. Chemical deterioration occurs when the chemical properties of an object react to heat or light. Brittleness in paper is a result of a chemical reaction within paper that was made using a sulfite pulping process. Until recently, most paper produced after 1860 has been manufactured in that way. The chemicals added to the paper (alum and rosin) form sulfuric acid when exposed to air and high temperatures. This alters the molecular structure of the paper, causing it to become embrittled. Paper that has undergone chemical deterioration is weakened and can be easily damaged—even to the extent of crumbling in one's hand.

Chemical deterioration often leads to physical deterioration, but physical deterioration is not dependent upon chemical deterioration. Careless handling of books and photographs can damage them. Poor storage conditions can result in exposure to insects or vermin that will destroy paper. Insects, such as silverfish, cockroaches, and beetles, and vermin, such as mice, rats, and squirrels, eat or gnaw on paper and leave droppings on materials. Careful consideration about where and how you store materials can extend their useful life.

◆ Provide a Stable Storage Environment

The primary means of protection is a stable environment. Such an environment—one that avoids fluctuations in temperature, relative humidity, and exposure to ultraviolet light—will slow chemical deterioration. Books, paper, computer disks, and phonograph records should be stored at 68°F and 45- to 55-percent relative humidity. Photographs, photographic film, and magnetic media require lower relative humidity of 30 to 40 percent. Above all, strive to maintain a stable, non-fluctuating temperature and relative humidity—especially relative humidity.

◆ Avoid Exposure to Light

Color and image fading are dependent on the intensity and duration of light exposure. Maintain low light conditions—store items away from direct sunlight and reduce exposure to other light sources. Do not expose documents to light for prolonged periods. Before storing your materials, consider their proximity to heat sources, such as radiators and heating vents.

◆ Avoid Exposure to Dust

Dust is another enemy of collections. If the storage site is not cleaned regularly, place the items in a box or other storage container to protect them from dust. It's a good idea to store materials in a container regardless of cleaning habits.

Storing materials in areas that meet the preceding guidelines will pay off in long-term preservation of the material.

Paper

Genealogists collect and generate a variety of paper records in the course of their research. Letters, newspaper clippings, birth certificates, marriage licenses, death certificates, and other legal documents, as well as photocopies and computer printouts, are paper based, and the paper is of varying quality. If the paper feels strong and flexible but tests acidic, it can be cleaned and deacidified prior to storage. De-acidification will not strengthen the paper, but it will stop chemical deterioration.

Paper Clips and Staples

Paper clips and staples can rust and leave marks on paper. They can also tear the document if not carefully removed. Bend paper clips open rather than sliding them off prior to any treatment. Plastic paper clips and non-rusting staples are available from archival catalogs.

Rubber bands can break down and leave a residue on valuable documents.

Surface Cleaning

Paper can be "dry cleaned" using an eraser or soft cleaning compound. A number of erasers and cleaning compounds are available commercially: Magic Rub™, Staedtler Mars Plastic, Dietzgen Skum-X™, Opaline Dry Cleaning Pad (see the appendix). This method works only for pencil marks and surface dirt.

There is no known method that will safely remove ink or grease stains from paper.

Figure 1. Roll the eraser bag between your fingers to shake out the cleanser.

1. With clean hands or, preferably, wearing white cotton gloves, work from the center to the outside edge, moving the eraser always toward the outside. Use a light touch; too much force can damage the paper. If you are using a cleaning compound contained in a bag, roll the bag between your fingers to release the eraser dust, rather than using the bag directly on the document; this prevents the dirt from being transferred from the document to the bag and onto the next document you clean (figure 1).

2. With clean fingers, gently rub the eraser filings over the document (figure 2).

3. Use a clean brush to remove the dirty eraser parts.

Testing for Acid and Deacidifying

Deacidify the paper after cleaning. To determine if deacidification is necessary for your document, do the following:

Figure 2. After shaking the eraser bag, gently rub the eraser filings with clean fingertips over the document.

1. Test the level of acidity with a pH pen—a felt-tip pen, usually chlorophenol red, used to test paper for alkalinity or acidity. These are available at low cost from many suppliers of archival-quality products (see the appendix). The pen may leave a mark, so select a corner or unobtrusive spot on the document. Place a small dot on the page with the pen (figure 3).

Figure 3. *Testing paper with a pH pen.*

2. Follow the manufacturer's instructions for interpreting the results. If acidic, consider deacidifying or photocopying the document. If alkaline, store in an acid-free, alkaline-buffered folder or envelope. (The material must be acid-free to stop deterioration and alkaline-buffered to prevent acid from adjacent items from transferring to the material; see the appendix for suppliers of acid-free, alkaline-buffered materials.)

3. Check acidic paper for ink colorfastness—whether the ink will retain its original hue without fading or running (it may bleed when deacidified). To test, wet a cotton swab with the deacidification solution and dab it on a small portion of the text (figure 4). If

Figure 4. *Testing paper for colorfastness prior to deacidifying.*

the ink bleeds or comes off on the swab, do not deacidify.

4. If you do not detect any bleeding, spray or brush the solution on the front of the document. (Be sure to work in a ventilated area.) Allow the document to dry and store it in an acid-free, alkaline-buffered folder, or encapsulate it (see below).

5. After cleaning and deacidifying, repair tears. Tears in paper should be repaired with archival-quality tape.

6. Consider encapsulation or photo-copying for damaged, brittle paper.

Encapsulation

Encapsulation is a reversible (meaning that it is not permanent) method of sealing a document between sheets of polyester—a static charge traps the paper between two transparent polyester sheets. This is not the same as lamination, a non-reversible process. The adhesive used in laminating can damage the document it is meant to protect. Encapsulation is especially useful for brittle materials because encapsulated brittle paper will not break when handled in an ordinary manner. Encapsulation is best done on single-page items. Books can be encapsulated, but they must be disbound (binding removed) and each page encapsulated separately.

Encapsulation materials are available from most suppliers of archival materials. The easiest method of encapsulation is to purchase precut sheets of polyester with double-sided tape already attached; you can purchase materials to customize to your own document. To encapsulate a document, do the following:

1. Deacidify the item. It is not essential to deacidify a document prior to encapsulation; however, deacidification slows chemical deterioration and is the preferred treatment of many conservators. (See the instructions above for deacidifying.)

2. Cut a sheet of polyester one inch larger than the document on all sides.

3. Wipe the polyester with a dust cloth to remove any lint and to create a static charge.

4. Center the document on one sheet of polyester, then place a weight on top of the document (figure 5).

5. Place double-sided tape along all four sides, leaving about ⅛ inch at each corner.

6. Remove the weight and center a second sheet of polyester the same size as the first on top of the document. Put the weight on top of the polyester "sandwich" you have created. Gently

Figure 5. *When encapsulating, cut polyester one inch larger than the document and place it on a flat surface. Center the document on top of the polyester; a weight holds it in place.*

Figure 6. *A second sheet of polyester covers the document being encapsulated; a weight holds the three layers in place. Remove the cover of the double-sided tape to seal the packet.*

move a brayer (roller) across the top of the document to remove any air bubbles. (A rolling pin is a good substitute brayer.)

7. Remove the cover over the double sided tape on the edges of the polyester and seal in place (figure 6). Remove the weight.

8. Once more, gently move a brayer across the top of the document to secure the seal (figure 7).

Photocopying

Another method of preserving brittle or acidic materials is to photocopy the document onto acid-free, alkaline-buffered paper. Many photocopy centers and archival supply companies sell this paper. Photocopying, however, will preserve only the intellectual or written contents of the document. If the physical object itself, such as a marriage license, has great value to you, consider encapsulating it to retain and protect it. You may want to consult a conservator for advice.

Figure 7. *Use a rolling pin or brayer to seal the encapsulation and push air out of the packet.*

Flattening and Storage

Paper should always be stored flat—never folded or rolled. Place papers in acid-free, alkaline-buffered folders or envelopes and store them out of direct light in the proper environment.

Rolled or folded paper should be flattened prior to treatment and storage. An easy way to flatten a paper item without placing undue stress on it is to humidify it, as explained below.

1. Place a wet sponge in a container with the item to be flattened resting on a rack or tray above the sponge. Tightly cover the container and leave it for a few hours or overnight.

2. After the paper becomes more pliable (because of the increased moisture content), carefully open it; do not force it. If there is still resistance, return it to the container.

3. When the document has relaxed and is easy to open, place it on top of a blotter or blotting paper covered with polyester web (see glossary). If the document was rolled, place it with the inside of the roll face down. Cover it with another blotter or polyester web and place light weights on the pile.

4. Allow the item to remain this way until the paper flattens.

Encapsulated paper does not need to be placed in acid-free containers, but it should be stored away from light.

Tall, rolled items can be humidified in a chamber constructed by placing a plastic trash container inside a larger, deeper trash container. Fill the bottom of the larger container with several inches of water, place the rolled documents inside the smaller container, and cover the large container. When the paper has relaxed, flatten it as described at left.

Books

Preparing for Storage

Books, both printed and manuscripts, and scrapbooks can be treated with techniques similar to those used with paper. Store them in identical environments (68°F, 45- to 50-percent relative humidity, limited light exposure). Remove paper clips and adhesive stickers before storing any book. Torn pages can be repaired with archival tape (figure 8), and surface cleaning can be performed on books that are not fragile or brittle.

Deacidifying

Books can be deacidified, but the process is slow because each page must be treated. Follow the guidelines listed above in the section on paper to decide if a book should be treated.

When deacidifying a book, place a sheet of polyester slightly larger than the book under the pages that you are treating (figure 9).

Place the polyester under each page as you spray, changing the polyester frequently to prevent a gummy residue from forming; this will protect the binding from an excessive buildup of deacidification solution. Because the deacidification formula permeates the paper, it is not necessary to spray both the front and back of a page.

Never attempt to repair on your own anything more than a paper tear in a book . If the item has high artifactual or sentimental value, consider having a conservator repair it.

Figure 8. *Apply archival tape to one side of a torn page and gently rub in place.*

Figure 9. *Place polyester under the page to prevent buildup of deacidifying solution.*

Photocopying

If you want only to preserve the information in a book and are not concerned about appearance, consider photocopying. If you decide to make a photocopy, use a copy machine with the glass platen close to or at the edge of the machine; this will allow you to copy all of the text on a page without forcing the book open. "Book friendly" photocopiers can be found in some college and university libraries.

Never force a book open flat to copy it; this will damage it and, if the book is brittle, it will not be repairable.

Some books may appear to be in good condition but cannot stand up to the prolonged handling of photocopying, so consider carefully before using this treatment option. There are professional preservation photocopying services that can make high-quality photocopies of books and provide bound copies (see appendix); the service may or may not disbind the book to photocopy it. If a book is extremely brittle and you wish to retain it, the best option may be to have it professionally photocopied and keep the original in an archival box.

Be aware that books that have been disbound for copying usually cannot be rebound.

Storage

Shelved books should stand upright—never leaning. Leaning places stress on the joint, or hinge, where the covers (boards) meet the spine and can break the binding. Use sturdy bookends that are at least half the height of the books they support. Always shelve heavy volumes with the spine down. Otherwise, the weight of the text block (pages) can cause the text block to pull out of the cover. To remove a book from a shelf, grasp it midway down the spine. Never pull on the headband at the top of the spine—it may break (see figure 10).

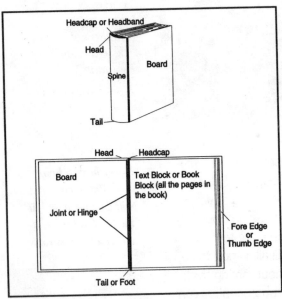

Figure 10. Parts of a book.

If a book is already damaged (detached covers and pages, weak joints), it can be tied together or placed in an acid-free, alkaline-buffered box. To tie a book, use unbleached heavy cotton string or tape and tie it around the book (figure 11), placing the knot at the top or the fore edge (figure 12)—the edge opposite the spine (making it easier to shelve the book than if the knot were on the front or back cover). Cotton string and tape are available through preservation catalogs.

Storage boxes are available commercially, but those made of lightweight paper board may not be strong enough to hold the weight of a book, so consider purchasing heavier boxes. Conservators also make customized boxes.

Figure 11. Tying a book with cotton tape.

Scrapbooks

Scrapbooks require special treatment. They are bound like books but are made up of various items attached to the pages. Deacidification is not always an option because a scrapbook may contain items that are not colorfast.

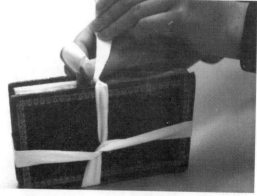

Figure 12. Tie the cotton tape so that the knot is on the fore edge. Be careful not to tie too tightly or the edge of the book will bend where the tape contacts it.

"Interleaving," however, is usually possible: place a sheet of acid-free, alkaline-buffered paper or polyester between each page; this will reduce acid migration to adjacent pages, but it will not stop the vapor action of acid from affecting the scrapbook. It is best to consult a conservator regarding the preservation of such a unique item.

Photographs

Just as do books and paper, photographs need special environmental conditions for proper long-term storage. The temperature should not exceed 68°F, and the relative humidity should be kept around 30 to 40 percent. High humidity (70 percent) can cause mold growth in some photographs. The possibility of chemical deterioration, which leads to fading, also increases with high humidity.

♦ Limit exposure to light—especially for color prints, slides, and negatives.

♦ Always handle photographs and negatives by their edges and wear white cotton or nylon lint-free gloves (figure 13).

♦ Be careful not to scratch photographs or negatives.

Figure 13. *Handling a photograph with lint-free gloves.*

Storage

Photographs can be stored in plastic or paper envelopes—or, more precisely, "enclosures"; each has advantages and disadvantages. Plastic enclosures made of polyethylene, polypropylene, and—the best of the three—uncoated polyester protect photos from fingerprints while allowing them to be viewed.

Paper enclosures protect the photograph but require that the photo be removed from the enclosure for viewing. They also cost less. Paper enclosures should be acid-free and contain no lignin, groundwood, or alum rosin sizing, nor should they be alkaline-buffered. Selec enclosures that have side seams; if the seam is elsewhere in the enclosure, keep the emulsion side (image side) of the photo away from the seam. If the collection will be handled often, it may be better to use plastic enclosures for the added protection they provide. Photos in either kind of enclosure should be stored in acid-free, alkaline-buffered boxes flat or on their sides. If the photos or negatives are heavy, store them on their sides.

Never deacidify photographs! They are quite different from books and paper, and are adversely affected by deacidification.

Photo Albums

Photo albums should be made of acid-free pages with slits cut to hold the photographs or with polyester pockets for holding individual photographs.

Writing on the front or back of a photograph is not advisable, but, if you must do so, write on the back using a special pen made for writing on photographs (see the appendix). Also consider writing on an acid-free slip of paper and storing it with the photo in a plastic enclosure, or writing directly on a paper enclosure or on the pages of a photo album.

Avoid self-adhesive pages with plastic page protectors (sometimes called magnetic photo albums); the adhesive is not acid-free and can damage photographs. Likewise, avoid rubber cement and other non-archival adhesives.

Old, scrapbook-type photo albums can be interleaved with acid-free paper or polyester film, which will provide support. Be aware that, if too many interleaves are inserted, the added pages will create pressure on the spine and can cause damage. If the scrapbook bulges from the added interleaving, remove enough so it lies flat again. Store all photo albums flat in boxes to protect them from dust.

Never attach an adhesive label to a photo (front or back); the glue will break down and get on nearby prints, to say nothing of what it could do to the photograph.

Special Needs

Consult a photographic conservator if you detect active deterioration.

Photographs made with very early photographic processes, such as daguerreotypes, ambrotypes, and tintypes, if still in their original cases, should be housed in acid-free boxes for extra protection. If they are not encased, place them in acid-free enclosures.

Photographs made with modern photographic processes, such as self-developing instant prints, should be stored separately from other photographs. These prints are generally smaller and can be damaged by the larger photographs in a collection, or, with their sharp edges can scratch unprotected photos.

There is the slight danger that the developing chemicals sealed inside instant prints could leak (both those sealed in their own plastic cases and peel-away prints).

Storing Negatives

Negatives should be stored in acid-free, alkaline-buffered paper enclosures to protect them from light. Envelopes made of glassine (a thin; transparent paper) are not recommended for long-term storage.

If you are unsure if you have nitrate negatives, take them to a reputable camera dealer for advice. If you cannot identify the film base, or if you suspect it may be cellulose nitrate or cellulose acetate, contact a photographic conservator for advice.

Negatives made of cellulose nitrate (used commonly until the 1950s) are highly flammable. Separate them from a collection, have them duplicated, and dispose of the originals.

Cellulose acetate (safety film) is subject to a type of chemical deterioration known as "vinegar syndrome" because of the strong, vinegary smell it gives off during decomposition. Store these negatives separately at low temperatures (40°F) to avoid deterioration and the loss of other negatives if deterioration does occur.

Motion Picture Film

Motion picture film presents many of the same preservation concerns as do photographic negatives.

A popular service offered by many camera stores is copying Super 8 and 16mm films onto videotape. This measure provides easy playback, but it is only a short-term preservation solution. Videotape (discussed in the next section) also has limitations. For that reason, if you copy polyester-based film to videotape, do not discard the film. Store it in a cool, dry place.

Cellulose nitrate film should be discarded. Cellulose acetate can be kept but only if it is stored away from other materials in low humidity and cool temperatures to avoid "vinegar syndrome." Remove film stored in metal cans and place it in acid-free boxes.

If you suspect that film is of cellulose nitrate or cellulose acetate (safety film), contact a photographic conservator for advice on how to save the image.

Videotape

Before storing a video cassette tape, be sure to break off the protection tab on the cassette to avoid accidental erasure.

Videotape presents two preservation problems: preserving the tape and preserving the playback machine. If you have a tape that you want to preserve, make a copy (at standard speed) and store the original. Each time a tape is played, the tape heads of the playback machine abrade the tape; this can eventually result in loss of image or sound. By storing the original, you insure that it can be copied again if the playback copy wears out. Standard speed offers the lowest recording density; using it allows a better chance for recovery should the tape be damaged.

Keep playback machines, such as video cassette recorders, clean and free of dust. Use professional-quality cleaning cassettes to clean the tape heads.

A tape should never be stopped in the middle of play and stored, nor should a tape be left in a playback machine when not in use.

There is much debate as to whether tapes should be rewound prior to storage. As a rule, do not rewind a tape until it is to be replayed.

◆ Return tapes to their boxes for storage, placing them upright on the short edge.
◆ Always store tapes vertically. (Storing tapes in the horizontal playing position can damage the tape edge over time).
◆ Keep cassettes dust-free, and never touch the tape inside the cassette.
◆ The storage temperature should never exceed 68°F or 30- to 40-percent relative humidity.

Sound Recordings

These comments are restricted to phonograph records and audio cassettes. Sound recordings for consumer use are not produced with materials intended for long-term storage. Maintaining an older playback machine is also a problem.

Phonograph Records

Keep phonograph record players free of dust and the stylus clean. Use a soft brush to clean the stylus by brushing from back to front.

Handling

◆ Keep phonograph records clean and dust-free.
◆ Always handle records by the outer edges or label to avoid leaving fingerprints and oils.

Storage

◆ Store phonograph records away from light and high temperatures, preferably no higher than 68°F and 50-percent relative humidity.
◆ Always remove phonograph records from the turntable.
◆ Always shelve phonograph records upright on their edges—never flat.

Phonograph records can be stored in their original dust jackets, but any shrink-wrapped plastic should be removed. Replace the original

For other types of sound recordings—such as wire recordings and wax cylinder recordings—consult a conservator who specializes in preserving early sound recordings.

Never attempt to blow dust off the stylus or record; it can cause the dust particles to become imbedded.

Do not allow phonograph records to lean when stored upright; it may cause warpage.

liner with a polyethylene sleeve. If the original liner contains textual information, photocopy it onto acid-free paper and store it with the disk.

Many archival supply companies sell boxes that can be used to store records upright and protected from dust and light.

Cleaning

Never use alcohol solutions; they can cause chemical deterioration. If a disk is extremely dirty, contact a conservator for further advice.

Clean records by using a soft, lint-free cloth moved in a circular direction along the grooves. Commercial cleaners are available that allow safe "deep cleaning" of records. Extremely dirty records can be washed with a soft terry cloth in warm water and a mild detergent. Blot dry immediately with a soft cloth to prevent water stains.

Audiotapes

The most common problem with tape machines is magnetized heads, which cause tapes to deteriorate and erase data. Repair shops can demagnetize tape heads.

Storage

Never store a tape that has been stopped in the middle; play the tape to the end or rewind it. Do not touch the tape with your fingers.

- ◆ Store audiotapes in a clean, dust-free environment of 68°F and 30- to 40-percent relative humidity.
- ◆ Always store tape in a covered container.
- ◆ If the tape is on a reel, be sure that the tape "pack" is even before storing it.

Cleaning

◆ Keep the playback machine clean and dust-free.

◆ Use commercial tape cleaners to clean the tape heads. You can also use 70-percent or higher isopropyl alcohol and a cotton swab.

Never clean the rubber rollers with alcohol, however. Clean them with water.

Creating a Backup

If a tape contains unique information, make a copy and store the original in a proper place. Use the copy for playback. Audiotapes, like videotapes, suffer abrasion from the play-back machine. A "use" copy allows the original to be preserved. When the use copy wears out, the original can be used to make another copy. You may also wish to make a transcript of the tape's contents and store the paper copy as well. Then, if you do not have access to a play-back machine, you will have, at the very least, a transcript of the information.

Computer Disks

Computer disks, whether they contain original research data or software, should always be backed up (copied) and the back-up copy stored away from the original— preferably off-site.

Like most researchers, genealogists have taken advantage of computers to aid their research. Computer storage disks have unique preservation needs.

Computer disks are not designed for permanent storage, so it is wise to print out important family history data stored on disk on acid-free, alkaline-buffered paper and store it in a safe place (in addition to a disk backup). Also, when upgrading hardware and software, transfer data files to the new medium or version of software so they will remain accessible.

Handling

Many of the same guidelines listed for audiotapes and videotapes apply to computer disks:

- ◆ Do not touch the disk.
- ◆ Keep the tape clean and in a protective box or plastic sleeve.
- ◆ Keep the playback machine (computer) clean and dust-free.
- ◆ Always make a backup copy.

A word of caution is in order for all formats that are dependent upon a machine (video cassette recorder, computer, cassette player) for retrieving the information. Technology is constantly changing and evolving, resulting in machine obsolescence. Home movie projectors have given way to the videotape player—and who knows what will replace it? Cassette players have replaced reel-to-reel tape recorders, and cassette players are being overtaken by digital audiotapes. Before re-recording movies or sound recordings in a new format, realize that this new technology also has pitfalls.

What can be done to provide for future playback? Maintain the playback machine in good working order. If you switch formats, re-record your film or tapes with the newer technology—but do not discard the originals. Something even better may come along, and copying from the original is always better than copying from a copy.

The tape you record on today's camcorder may not be playable ten or twenty years from now unless you also keep the video cassette recorder.

TEXTILES

Textiles come in many forms: embroidery samplers, keepsake handkerchiefs, quilts, wedding dresses, baptismal gowns, and military uniforms, to name a few. They may be made of synthetic or natural fibers, but all require the same storage considerations. Textiles must be kept in stable environments out of extreme heat and humidity. They should not be exposed to light, nor should they be stored where they are vulnerable to insect or vermin damage.

Cleaning

If the item is old or fragile, consult a textile conservator—do not attempt to clean the item yourself.

If possible, a textile should be cleaned before storage. Stains can set and become harder to remove if they are left untreated.

For sturdy, colorfast textiles, hand wash using a very mild detergent. Allow the item to air dry by placing it on absorbent material and running a fan nearby. Note that cotton and linen fibers become stronger when wet, but silk becomes weaker. Use extreme care when hand washing.

Storage

How to store a textile depends on the size and strength of the item.

Flat Storage

Flat storage may be proper for a sampler or other small keepsake. Place it in a box to protect it from dust and light. If the item will be handled often, place it on a piece of acid-free cardboard. When removing the item from the box, simply lift the cardboard and transport the item on it.

Rolled Storage

Items that are too large to store flat—for example, a rug—can be rolled.

1. Roll the item carefully, using acid-free tissue paper to support the center and protect the fibers between layers.

2. Wrap it with muslin and tie it with acid-free string at the top, bottom, and middle sections of the roll. Tie large rolls in evenly spaced sections along the length of the roll.

Hanging Storage

If you decide to store a garment on a hanger, consider the following:

◆ Is the garment strong enough to be hung for a long period of time? The entire stress of hanging is at the shoulder seams. If the seams appear weak, store the garment flat in a container.

If possible, avoid folding a garment prior to storage. If folding is unavoidable, pad the folds with acid-free tissue. Creases in the garment should also be supported with acid-free tissue.

◆ Is there enough room in the closet in which the garment will be stored? Items should not be packed so tightly as to compress the fabric.

◆ Is the garment too long to hang in a closet? If it is, carefully drape the bottom of the garment over a second padded hanger.

◆ Always use padded hangers; the padding should not compress under the weight of the garment and should be wide enough to offer support on either side of the shoulder seam.

Do not cover the garment with a plastic garment bag (the plastic can create dust-attracting static electricity, and it may not be inert; over time, it could decompose, harming the items stored in the bag). Instead, wrap muslin around it to protect it from light and dust.

A final word about caring for textiles: Take pains to carefully store the garments and other textiles that you want to preserve for the next generation. If your wedding dress or your son's christening gown are packed away, get them out and check on their condition. Taking the extra time and expense to preserve the items now will ensure that the next generation and perhaps the one after will have the garments to enjoy. We inherit heirlooms, but we also create them.

DISASTER RECOVERY

Even if you have carefully stored your preservable materials, storms, leaks, floods, and fires can damage them. A few tips for recovering documents after such disasters follow. Remember, if a document is truly unique, make a copy and store the original in a suitable archival box off-site. If you decide to keep it in a safe-deposit box, ask about the temperature and humidity before committing it to permanent storage there.

If you decide to store your keepsakes outside your home:

The last place you should consider storing archival materials is a low-cost storage facility that has no temperature or humidity controls to protect your items. Further, items left there could be at risk for theft or disaster.

- ◆ Request a tour of the site.
- ◆ Ask about climate control. Is the air conditioning turned off on weekends, causing fluctuations in temperature and humidity?
- ◆ Ask about security. Is there someone who will make rounds when the facility is closed and who could detect a fire or leak in its early stages?
- ◆ Ask about liability. Are they willing to pay for restoration of materials damaged due to their negligence?

Recovery From Water Damage

The first thing to do when a disaster occurs is to stabilize the area to prevent further damage. This might mean throwing plastic over books, photos, or other items to protect them from an overhead leak or moving them to higher ground. After they have been stabilized, salvage the maximum amount of items. Remember that in a water-caused emergency—and fires should be included because water is used to put out a fire—you have 48 to 72 hours before mold begins to grow.

Air drying is a simple, low-tech method of drying books, papers, photographs, audiotape, videotape, computer disks, and textiles and is the preferred method for photographs. It works best on damp materials, but it can be used for saturated materials, though only if they can be completely dry within 72 hours. Always keep the air moving with fans.

Do not attempt to air-dry material that is dripping wet unless the temperature is 70 to 77°F or lower and the relative humidity is 50 percent or lower.

To air dry an item, cover a table or other flat work surface with plastic, and lay newsprint over this to absorb moisture. Change the newsprint when it becomes damp.

You can hang lightweight materials—pamphlets, file folders, paper, and photographs—to dry from monofilament lines (fishing line) stretched in six-foot lengths. Hang the items about half an inch apart.

To seperate a pile of wet papers, place a single sheet of polyester slightly larger than the papers you are attempting to seperate on top of the stack. Gently rub the polyester to create surface tension; this will cause the polyester to adhere to the top sheet of paper. Gently lift the polyester. The top sheet of wet paper will cling to the polyester and will be lifted from the wet stack. Hang the polyester (with the single sheet of paper attached) on a monofilament line or lay it on a nylon screen to dry.

To flatten a paper or photo while it is drying on a flat surface, do the following: When almost dry, interleave it between polyester web and blotting paper—use weights. Place a blotter on the bottom, with paper or photo on top, polyester web next, and then a weight. You can dry more than one item at a time with this method, but separate items with layers of web and blotting paper.

To dry a book:

1. Open it slightly and place it on its head (top edge). Put an eraser or styrofoam under one end and tilt it back, and put toothpicks in the hinge area to separate the boards from the text block.

2. After a saturated book has dried a bit, interleave it with absorbent paper every few pages. Interleaving should not exceed one-third of the book's thickness. Remove and replace the interleaving with dry paper when it becomes damp.

3. To prevent humidity from building in the drying area, remove wet papers

from the room often and run a dehumidifier if you can.

4. Reverse the books periodically from head to tail and front to back. Above all, never open a wet text block of a book—the paper may tear.

Freezing Books and Paper

If a large collection of books and papers becomes water damaged, they can be placed in a home freezer for storage until they can by dried individually—but only if the freezer operates in the -10 to -40°F range.

- ◆ Freezing should not be done with clay-coated papers (glossy paper).
- ◆ Freezing can take a long time.
- ◆ Materials will probably not return to their original condition

One benefit of freezing is that it gives you time to decide what to do next. Frozen items can be removed from the freezer and allowed to air dry a few at a time.

Another drying method which gives very good results is vacuum-freeze drying. Providers of this service can place frozen books and papers in a chamber, where a vacuum is created. Heat is then introduced and the items dry at temperatures below 32°F. The water passes from a frozen to a vapor state without becoming liquid. This process prevents additional swelling and distortion, though some swelling

Only books and paper can be frozen; never freeze film, photographs, or tape.

Use the vacuum-freeze dry process for photographs. Film-based items (photographic negatives, motion picture film) can be damaged, so consult a conservator before vacuum freeze drying film.

that occurs prior to freezing may remain. The process also brings dirt and mud to the surface, where it can be wiped off. Coated papers can be treated this way if done within six hours of the disaster. Vellum and leather may not survive the process; consult with the vendor before treating.

For a list of vendors who can provide this service, see the appendix. Photographic prints can be air dried but, if in doubt, you can contact the Information Center at Eastman Kodak Company for advice (see the appendix for address and telephone number).

Audiotape and Videotape Procedures

Audiotapes and videotapes should be allowed to air dry. If you have access to a tape cleaning machine, run the tape through it. After a tape has been cleaned, copy it onto another tape. Use the copy for playback and store the original. There are companies that will professionally restore tapes (see the appendix). It is wise to copy any unique item and to store the original in a safe, secure place.

Do not run a dirty tape cassette through a video cassette recorder or audio tape player to clean it; the dirt may be transferred to the machine heads and picked up by other tapes when they are played.

Soot and Ozone Treatments

Soot-covered books can be safely cleaned with a chemical sponge or clean cloth. Hold the book tightly closed and wipe off any soot or grime. Continue to clean it until the sponge or cloth remains unsoiled when passed over the item. Allow the item to air out in the sun.

If you are interested in passing a book or garment on to the next generation, avoid ozone treatment.

Ozone is often used after fires to remove lingering odors. However, ozone is a respiratory irritant and can speed the chemical deterioration of some materials. Before treating books or any item with ozone, consider how long you want to keep the items being treated.

Choosing A Conservator

This guide frequently suggests that you consult a conservator regarding complex treatment of documents. How do you find and select a conservator? The American Institute for Conservation of Historic and Artistic Works (AIC) publishes a leaflet titled "Guidelines for Selecting a Conservator," and AIC also runs a referral service. (This service is not intended to serve as a recommendation or an endorsement.) Another source for information about conservators is a local museum or university library.

Many individuals who call themselves conservators do not follow the code of ethics for conservators developed by AIC. Some library binders and photographers advertise conservation services, but be cautious when soliciting their services. Many of them are not true conservators, and the work they perform may do more harm than good.

A conservator can be expected to provide a customer with a written valuation of the necessary treatment and a cost estimate. A conservator should notify the customer if the prescribed treatment needs to be altered. Conservators should complete work in the agreed-upon time frame. The materials used should be stable and appropriate to the item being treated, and a conservator should provide security for a customer's items.

Before deciding on a conservator:

- Ask to see a sample of his or her work. How is the workmanship? Is it aesthetically pleasing?
- Ask to visit the conservator's workroom.
- Ask if he or she prescribes to the AIC Code of Ethics and Standards of Practice.

APPENDIX:
LIST OF SUPPLIERS

Absorene Company
1609 N. 14th St.
St. Louis, Missouri 63106
1-800-662-7399

Chemical sponges for cleaning fire-damaged materials; also sold under the name Dirt Eraser or Wall Bright at hardware stores.

American Institute for Conservation of Historic and Artistic Works
1400 16th St. NW, Suite 340
Washington, D.C. 20036
202-232-6636

Referrals for all types of conservation services (books, paper, photographs, fabric).

Archival Products
2134 E. Grand Ave.
Des Moines, Iowa 50317
515-262-3191
800-526-5640

Preservation photocopying; storage boxes.

Bill Cole Enterprises, Inc.
P.O. Box 60
Randolph, Maryland 02368-0060
617-986-2653
800-225-8248

Polyester.

BMS-CAT
1-800-433-2940

Disaster recovery services.

BookLab, Inc.
8403 Cross Park Dr., Suite 2E
Austin, Texas 78754
512-837-0479

Preservation photocopying and conservation services.

Custom Manufacturing, Inc.
P.O. Box 1215
Emmitsburg, Maryland 21727
717-642-6304
717-642-6596 FAX

Custom-made alkaline boxes.

Disaster Recovery Services, Inc.
414 Blue Smoke Court West
Ft. Worth, Texas 76105
1-800-856-3333

Disaster recovery services.

Eastman Kodak Company
Information Center
343 State St.
Rochester, New York 14650
800-242-2424

Advice on photographs, films.

Gaylord Brothers, Inc.
Box 4901
Syracuse, New York 13221-4901
800-448-6160

Archival supplies, deacidification spray, pH pens.

Heckman Bindery
One Heckman Square
P.O. Box 89 North
Manchester, Indiana 46962
1-800-334-3628

Custom made boxes, conservation and repair of books.

Image Permanence Institute
R.I.T. City Center
50 West Main St.
Rochester, New York 14614
716-475-5199

Advice on photographs, films.

Library of Congress
Preservation Information
and Education Office
LM-GO7 Washington, D.C. 20540
202-707-1840
202-707-5634 (conservation office)

Preservation and conservation advice.

Light Impressions Corporation
439 Monroe Ave.
P.O. Box 940
Rochester, New York 14603-0940
800-828-6216

Archival supplies, deacidification spray, pH pens.

Midwest Freeze/Dry, Ltd.
7236 North Central Park
Skokie, Illinois 60076
708-679-4756

Freeze dry preservation services.

National Archives and Records Administration
Preservation Officer
Washington, D.C. 20408
202-523-5496

Preservation and conservation advice.

Northeast Document Conservation Center
100 Brickstone Square
Andover, Massachusetts 01810-1428
508-470-1010

Preservation photocopying and conservation services.

Northstar
P.O. Box 409, Highway #371 N.
Nisswa, Minnesota 56468
218-963-2900
800-551-3223

Freeze-dry preservation services.

Ocker & Trapp Library Bindery, Inc.
17C Palisade Ave.
P.O. Box 229
Emerson, New Jersey 07630

Custom-made boxes, conservation services.

Rocky Mountain Regional Conservation Center
University of Denver
2420 South University Blvd.
Denver, Colorado 80208
303-733-2712

Preservation and conservation advice.

Southeastern Library Information Network (SOLINET)
Preservation Program
400 Colony Square, Plaza Level 1202
Peachtree St. NE
Atlanta, Georgia 30361
404-892-0943
800-999-8558

Preservation and conservation advice.

3M Film and Allied Products Division
3M Center
St. Paul, Minnesota 55101
612-733-1110

Advice regarding magnetic media.

University Products
517 Main St.
P.O. Box 101
Holyoke, Massachusetts 01041-0101
800-628-1912

Archival supplies, deacidification spray, pH pens.

VidiPax
920 Broadway
16th Floor
New York, New York 10010
800-653-8434

Video restoration, consulting, disaster services.

BIBLIOGRAPHY

Cassaro, James P. *Planning and Caring for Library Audio Facilities*. Music Library Association Technical Reports, Number 17. Canton, Mass.: Music Library Association, 1989.

Conservation DistList, various postings. For information, contact the following electronic mail address: consdist@lindy.stanford.edu

Davis, Nancy. *Handle With Care: Preserving Your Heirlooms*. Rochester, N.Y.: Rochester Museum and Science Center, 1991.

DePew, John N. *A Library, Media, and Archival Preservation Handbook*. ABC-CLIO: Santa Barbara, Calif., 1991.

Greenfield, Jane. *Books: Their Care and Repair*. New York: H.W. Wilson Company, 1983.

Henderson, Kathryn Luther, and William T. Henderson, eds. *Conserving and Preserving Materials in Nonbook Formats*. Urbana-Champaign, Ill.: University of Illinois, Graduate School of Library and Information Science, 1991.

Horton, Carolyn. *Cleaning and Preserving Bindings and Related Materials*. Chicago: American Library Association, 1976.

International Federation of Library Associations and Institutions Core Program on Preservation and Conservation. *Care, Handling, and Storage of Photographs*. IFLA Pac. Washington, D.C.: Library of Congress, 1992.

Reilly, Bernard F., Jr., James M. Reilly, Debbie Hess Norris, Steven T. Puglia, Paula De Stefano, Julia Van Haaften, and Patricia McClung. *Photograph Preservation and the Research Library*. Mountain View, Calif.: Research Libraries Group, 1991.

Reilly, James M. *Care and Identification of 19th-Century Photographic Prints*. Rochester, N.Y.: Eastman Kodak Company, 1986.

Ritzenthaler, Mary Lynn. *Preserving Archives and Manuscripts*. SAA Basic Manual Series. Chicago: Society of American Archivists, 1993.

____, Gerald J. Munoff and Margery S. Long. *Archives and Manuscripts: Administration of Photographic Collections*. SAA Basic Manual Series. Chicago: Society of American Archivists, 1984.

Ward, Alan. *A Manual of Sound Archive Administration*. Hants, England: Gower Publishing Co., 1990.

Waters, Peter. *Procedures for Salvage of Water-Damaged Library Materials*. Washington, D.C.: Library of Congress, 1975.

Wilhelm, Henry G., and Carol Brower. *The Permanence and Care of Color Photographs: Traditional and Digital Color Print, Color Negatives, Slides, and Motion Pictures*. Grinnell, Iowa: Preservation Publishing Co., 1993.

GLOSSARY

acid-free: description of material that has a pH level of 6.0 or higher; may also be alkaline-buffered.

acid migration: the transfer of acid through direct contact or vapor transfer.

alkaline-buffered: material that has a calcium carbonate "buffer," which prevents acid migration.

alum rosin sizing: a sizing method introduced in mid-1800s paper production that has resulted in widespread embrittlement of paper. Alum was added to the rosin sizing to insure uniform distribution of the sizing agent. Over time, the alum reacts with air and water to form sulfuric acid in paper. Acid leads to embrittlement or chemical deterioration.

board: The cover of a book.

book block: See text block.

brittle paper: paper that breaks with two double folds or less on the same corner. Brittleness is caused by alum rosin sizing. Brittle paper is fragile, and repairs to it should never be attempted.

chemical sponge: natural, reusable sponge used for cleaning books after a fire.

deacidification: a process to neutralize acid in books or paper documents by applying a solution that neutralizes acid and leaves an alkaline reserve to prevent further acid buildup.

encapsulation: a reversible process of enclosing a single sheet of paper between two pieces of polyester and sealing with double-sided tape (or ultrasonic welding). The polyester creates a static charge and holds the document in place. This is an excellent treatment for brittle paper. (It is not the same as lamination, a non-reversible and unadvised treatment.)

enclosure: any object used to house or enclose another object to protect it from harmful elements, such as light, dust, insects, etc. Archival boxes, acid-free envelopes, and polyester sleeves are types of enclosures used in preservation.

fore edge: on a book, the edge opposite the spine; the side of the book that opens up. A book should never be shelved on its fore edge. Also called the thumb edge.

foot: See tail.

head: on a book, the top edge.

headband: on a book, the strip of colored cloth tape at the head and tail of the spine. A book should never be removed from a shelf by pulling on the headband—it may tear. Also called a headcap.

hinge: See joint.

joint: on a book, where the covers (boards) meet the spine. Also known as the hinge.

lignin: substance found in wood which provides structural strength in a tree; undesirable element in paper and boxes made for long-term storage.

Mylar ™: a trade name for polyester.

pH pen: a felt-tip pen, usually chlorophenol red, used to test paper for alkalinity or acidity.

playback machine: a machine used to play back stored information. For example, a record player is a playback machine for phonograph records; a video cassette recorder is a playback machine for videotapes.

polyester: a stable plastic used for archival sleeves or to encapsulate items. Mylar™ is the name of one brand of polyester.

polyester web: generic term for strong, lightweight polyester material used to support wet paper; available in fabric stores as "non-fusible interfacing."

sizing: A glutinous material used to fill the pores of paper, textiles, and other materials.

spine: the bound edge of a book; usually the book's title appears on the spine.

tail: on a book, the bottom edge; also called the foot.

text block: the body of a book, consisting of all the pages. Often called the book block.

thumb edge: See fore edge.

The author, Barbara Sagraves.

BIOGRAPHY

Barbara Sagraves lives with her husband and son in Chicago and works in the Preservation Department of Northwestern University Library. She has a masters degree in medieval history from Michigan State University and an MLIS (master of library science) from the University of Michigan. She has taught preservation at the Rosary College Graduate School of Library and Information Science and done preservation consulting in the Chicago area.